TENNIS

Improving is Fun

BY

CLAY J. MIZE

USPTA PROFESSIONAL

FOUNDER – KAIZEN TENNIS

Tennis
Improving is Fun
Published by Thorn Hill Books
117 Lakewood Drive
Sheffield, AL 35660

ISBN-13: 978-1095075692
© 2019 by Clay Mize

THORN HILL
BOOKS

Acknowledgements

I would like to express my appreciation to my friends and mentors in tennis who have helped me to be a better teacher and coach. My most notable mentors have been through their tireless efforts to teach the game of tennis. The are as follows: Rick Macci of Macci Tennis Academy, Nick Bolletri of The Bollertri Academy, Patrick Dougherty of IMG Academy, Craig O'Shanessey of Brain Game Tennis, Brad Gilbert and his excellent book on Winning Ugly, Bill Belser, Jorge Capastany of Hope Academy, Jeff Salzenstein of Tennis Evolution, Paul Wardlaw of High Percentage Tennis and countless other USPTA professionals from whom I have had the privilege to learn.

I would also like to thank the USPTA and USTA for the great resources they provide to teaching professionals.

Table of Contents

SECTION I

CHAPTER 1

About Kaizen Tennis

"There is no way around hard work. Embrace it. You have to put in the hours because there's always something which you can improve." –Roger Federer, The greatest tennis player of all time

The word Kaizen is a Japanese word meaning **continuous improvement.** The word became popular when American and Japanese companies began implementing this approach and philosophy to their businesses. The idea is that no matter where we are in our development, we can always improve.

It is the same way with Tennis. We can always improve, and there is a secret hidden in this philosophy. The secret is that the attitude of continuous improvement makes the game more and more fun.

In many ways tennis is like the Martial Arts. Tennis is a game of very distinct movements. The student must learn to master these movements if he or she wishes to become proficient as an all court player.

Our approach is designed to give the student fun short-term goals that progress over time into a total game. We believe this approach keeps the student motivated as their knowledge, confidence and mastery over the various movements and strokes of the game grow.

We have ten levels toward tennis mastery. If the student passes all ten levels, they will essentially be an all court tennis player that has a mastery over the entire game equivalent to a black belt in Karate.

Like Martial Arts uses a belt system, we use an armband system. Each armband color represents a level of mastery.

Here is a summary of the armband levels...

Level 1 - White - Beginner

Level 2 - Pink - Rules and basic strokes.

Level 3 - Green - More rules, perspective, sportsmanship, more strokes and controlling direction.

Level 4 - Red - Mental toughness, physical training, beginning strategies, stroke consistency.

Level 5 - Orange - Increased mental, physical, strategic and decision making, stroke variations and greater precision.

Level 6 - Blue – Available after level 4 achieved.

Level 7 - Brown – Available after level 4 achieved.

Level 8 - Purple - Available after level 6 achieved.

Level 9 - Gold - Available after level 6 achieved.

Level 10 - Black - Available after level 8 achieved.

Levels 6 and 7 competencies and study materials will be available to the student once they reach level 4 red. Levels 8 and 9 competencies and study materials will be available to the student once they reach level 6 blue. Black competencies and study materials will be available to the student once they reach level 8 purple.

The Power of Yet

The power of yet is the **attitude for success** needed in tennis. No player starts out good at tennis. Instead of saying and thinking, "I am not good at tennis," we should think or say "I am not good, yet. Tennis is similar to learning to play an instrument like the piano or guitar. It takes a lot of practice to be good.

Goal Setting

Goal setting is important to making improvement. The arm-band system makes goal setting easy, as the next arm-band level is always a good goal to achieve. To again quote Roger Federer, "You have to believe in the long-term plan you have, but you need the short-term goals to motivate and inspire you."

A Sport for Ladies and Gentlemen

Tennis has a tradition for being a sport for ladies and gentlemen. Because of this it is important that each player learn not only the rule of tennis, but also the etiquette of tennis.

Tennis is a sport which strives to cultivate an atmosphere of congeniality and respect. It should be an atmosphere where all players feel safe and comfortable.

This means always showing respect for coaches, tournament officials, fellow players and partners. Show good sportsmanship in all competitive situations.

CHAPTER 2

Tennis is Like Life

Tennis uses the language of life… advantage, service, fault, break, love….every match is a life in miniature. -- Andre Aggasi

Tennis is a great game and lots of fun, but it is not an easy game. To be good at tennis, like other skills such as piano or basketball, it can take many years of practice. However, you can be sure that the harder you work on your game and don't quit, the better you will become.

There are lots of benefits to the one who learns to play tennis. Tennis will help you improve your hand-eye coordination, your agility and gracefulness, your endurance and even help to shape your body into a more "in shape" person.

This book will help you to understand how the game of tennis is played and will make you an expert on the rules.

CHAPTER 3

The Racquet

The following is the parts of a racquet...

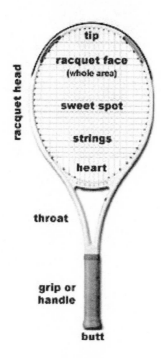

The Handle

The handle is an octagon having eight sides. Notice that each side has a number. The sides and numbers will be an important point when we talk later about how to grip the racquet. The "one" position is on top with the edge of the racquet pointing upward instead of lying flat. See below.

CHAPTER 4

Keeping Score

Each point and game is started with a serve from behind the baseline (See diagram of the court on page 15. The server gets two tries to hit the serve into the service box. The first serve in a game starts on the right side of the centerline and is served diagonally into the service box on the left side. After the first point, the server will then serve from the left of the center line into the service box on the right side. The server changes from side to side after each point.

Scoring in tennis may seem a little complicated, and it is until you play a few matches. The entire contest is called a match. A match is made up of sets. Sets are made up of games. Games are made up of points.

Scoring a game starts as follows...

Love, 15, 30, 40 Game point. The word "Love" is the same as zero. If both players reach 40 points, a player must win two points in a row to win the game. Another name for the score 40/40 is deuce.

Whoever wins the first point after the score reaches deuce it is said to be their advantage. If the server wins the point, the score is "advantage server." If the receiver wins the next point after deuce, the score is "advantage receiver." If the player wins a point when it is not his advantage, then the score goes back to deuce and a player must again win two points in a row.

Set Scoring

Tennis games are played within what is called a set. A traditional set is six games. To win a set, a player must be the first to win six games and must be ahead by two games to win the set. For example, the set is over if the score reaches six games to four games. However, if both players are tied at five games each then they continue to play till one player has a two-game advantage.

Alternative Scoring to Speed Up the Game

Today, many tournament directors will speed up the game by calling for a tie breaker once the set score reaches six games each (Six games all is another way of saying this). When this happens, the players will play a unique game called a tie-breaker. We will get into tiebreaker scoring at a later time.

Match Scoring

In traditional scoring, a player must win 2 out of 3 sets to win a match. Whoever wins the match has won the contest. (At the professional level there are times in men's tennis when the match consists of winning 3 out of 5 sets).

High School Scoring

At the high school level, the organizers have shortened the format for playing a match. A "pro set" is a match made up of eight games. If the score is tied at 8 games each, a tiebreaker will be played to decide the winner.

Tiebreaker

There is more than one method to score a tiebreaker. However, most high schools use the 7-point tiebreaker method. The tiebreaker game is the first player to win seven points and with a margin of two points. The winner of the tiebreaker wins the set and the match.

Who Starts the Serve on the Tiebreaker?

Since the score is tied and the winner of the tiebreaker game wins the set, it is important to know who serves first. The player to serve first is the player who was the receiver in the last game. The person who served last will be the receiver.

How to Play a Tiebreaker

Player one serves the first point, and the serve goes over to player two. After the first point, each player will serve two times and switch servers till the tiebreaker is complete. The player that reaches 7 points first with a 2-point margin wins the tiebreaker. Additional rules for a tiebreaker will be covered later.

No Ad Scoring

Another way that high schools have used to speed up a match is no-ad game scoring. Once both players reach a score of 40/40 the next point decides the game. This type of scoring makes the games go much faster and is useful when a high school team has limited time to finish a match.

CHAPTER 5

The Court

The following is a diagram of a tennis court.

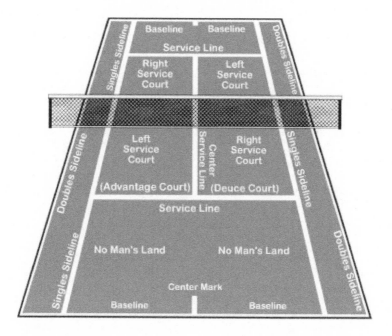

About the Court

Tennis courts are usually designed to play both singles (one person on each side of the court) or doubles (two people on each side of the court) separated by a net. The doubles court is larger than the singles court. The outside lines are the doubles sideline, and the inside lines are for singles. The area between the singles and doubles sidelines if often called "the doubles alley."

On each end of the court is the baseline that is dissected by a center mark. The line between the baseline and the net is known as the service line. If the serve goes beyond this line, then the serve is "out."

The area between the baseline and the service line is often called "no man's land." This is not the official name of this area but is called that by so many tennis teachers that the name has stuck. Of course, players can stand in this area, however, because so many balls fall in this area of the court it would mean you are trying to hit balls that are falling at your feet and that is very difficult to hit, thus the name "no man's land."

Finally, the "center line" separates the left service box (deuce court) from the right service box (advantage court).

A player is not restricted to staying inside the tennis court lines. He can be anywhere he likes inside or outside the tennis court lines as he moves to hit a ball.

The Net

The net that separates the players is 36 inches tall in the middle and slopes up till it reaches the net posts on each side. The net height at the net posts is 42 inches high.

No player may touch the net during a point. If a person touches the net during a point, she loses that point. Neither can a person hit a ball before it crosses the net. If they do, the point goes to the other person or team.

CHAPTER 6

Playing a Match

Before the First Game Begins

Before the game begins, the players must decide on who will serve first. This can be done by flipping a coin or is usually done by flipping the racquet and calling up or down using the logo on the butt of the racquet.

For example, the Wilson racquet has a large W on the butt of the racquet. So, when using a Wilson racquet, one person would spin the racquet, and the other would call out either W or M (M being an upside-down W). The winner then has the choice of serving first, receiving first or which side of the court they wish to begin on. If the winner decides to receive or serve first, the other person can choose which side to begin playing on.

Changing Sides

After the first game is complete, the players will change ends of the court and continue to change ends on odd-numbered games. So, for example, players will change on the first, third, fifth, seventh game, etc. till the set is complete.

When players change ends of the court, they have 90 seconds to rest before the next game begins. Most players take this time to sit, drink water and towel off if they are sweating.

Before Beginning the Game with a Serve

Before making the first serve, the server should have two balls with him since the server gets two tries to make a good serve. One ball should be in his/her pocket and the other in his hand ready to serve. Some players only take one ball, and if they miss it, they have to interrupt play to find another ball. This is very discourteous and slows down the pace of the game.

Starting the Game

The server must stand behind the baseline before each serve. Her foot must not be touching the line. On the very first serve of a new game, the server stands to the right of the center mark and serves into the left service court also known as the deuce court. She will then alternate serving into the advantage and deuce court with each serve.

If the serve goes beyond the service line on the opposite court, the ball is ruled "out" and is called a "fault." The server gets one additional serve. If the server misses the second serve by not landing it in the service box, then the server loses that point and moves to the other side of the center mark and begins a new point by serving. It is a double fault when neither the first or second serves goes in.

If the ball lands on the line of the service box the serve is considered to be "in," and the point has begun. It is the receiver's responsibility to call whether the serve is "in" or "out" and is part of the reason the game is known as a game for ladies and gentlemen.

It is the responsibility of each player to call whether a ball is in or out on his side of the court. This responsibility of calling the ball in or out tests a person's integrity and sportsmanship when a shot is close to the line and the player is unsure if the ball is in or out.

If the player is unsure if the ball is in or out, he/she should give their playing opponent the benefit of the doubt and call the ball "in." This requires a person to be a "lady" or "gentlemen" in his/her heart.

The Toss

Every serve starts with a toss. A player is not required to hit a serve if they feel uncomfortable with their toss. They can continue to toss the ball as many times as they wish till they like the toss. However, all players should practice their toss until they can toss it consistently.

Serving and the Net

If a ball skims the top of the net on the service and lands outside the service box, it is a fault. However, if it skims the net and lands in the service box, it is called a "let." A "let" on service means that the server must re-serve. If a "let" occurs on the first serve then the server gets two more serves. However, if a "let" occurs on the second serve the server only gets one additional serve.

However, the server gets to re-serve every time a "let" occurs with no limitation. In other words, if the server serves a let three times in a row, he will continue to get another serve.

Keeping the Score

The Set Score

It is the server's responsibility to call out the set score before the beginning of a new game. If the server calls out a set score and the receiver does not agree with it, he/she should call time out and discuss the discrepancy.

Game Score

The server is also required to call out the game score before every serve. Again, If the server calls out the game score and the receiver does not agree with it, she should call time out and discuss the discrepancy. Calling out the score before each point cuts down on players forgetting the game score.

When calling out the game score, the server calls out the server's score first, and then the receiver's score. For example, if the server has won one point and the receiver none, the server would call out the score as 15/love. If the receiver had won the first point, the server would have called out love/15.

More Help Keeping up with Game Score

Another way to help the server keep up with the game score is by which service box he is serving to. If the server is serving into the left service box (deuce court) it must be an **even-numbered** score.

For example, all the following scores would indicate you are into the left deuce court. The score is **Love/Love** (O points for either player) **15/15** (1 point for each player or a total of 2 points), **30/30** (2 points for each player or a total of 4 points) **40/40** (3 points for each player or a total of 6 points). **40/15** or **15/40** (3 points for one player and 1 point for the other player for a total of 4 points) 0/**30** or **30**/0 (0 points for one player and 2 points for the other player or a total of 2 points.

If the server is serving into the right service box (advantage court) the game score must be an **odd-numbered** point. For example, if the score is **Love/15 or 15/Love** (O points for one player and 1 point for the other totaling 1 point) **15/30 or 30/15** (1 point for one player and two for the other or a total of 3 points), **30/40 or 40/30** (2 points for one player and 3 points for the other or a total of 5 points)

Knowing this comes in handy when the server calls out a score but has lined up to serve into the wrong service box for that score. Both server and receiver should know this is time to call time out and clarify the game score. For example, if the server calls the score 40/15, which is a total of 4 points, but lines up to serve into the advantage court (right side), then you know that either the server is lining up wrong or the score is wrong. The receiver should call time out to discuss the error.

After each game, the players should adjust the set scorekeeper usually mounted on the net post. See below:

Receiving or Returning a Serve

The receiver usually stands near the baseline to receive the serve in the ready position (See below). If she serves hard and deep, the receiver might want to back up behind the baseline a foot or two. However, if the server serves slower, the receiver might want to step inside the baseline a few steps to receive the serve. The receiver should never stand inside the service box.

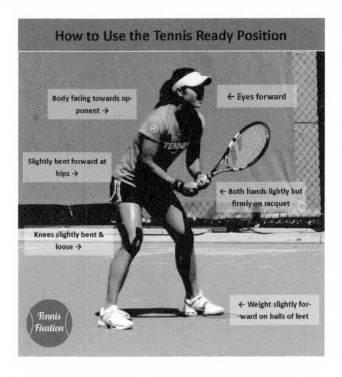

How to Use the Tennis Ready Position

Body facing towards opponent →

← Eyes forward

Slightly bent forward at hips →

← Both hands lightly but firmly on racquet

Knees slightly bent & loose →

← Weight slightly forward on balls of feet

Tennis Fixation

When you receive a serve, it is your responsibility to call the ball "out" immediately if the ball does not land in the service box or on the line. You must let the serve bounce in the service box before hitting the "return of serve." Taking the ball in the air before it hits in the service box is not allowed. Also, if the ball hits the returner before hitting the ground, even if the serve would have been outside the service box, it is the server's point.

Number of Bounces

The ball can only bounce once on your side of the court before you must hit and send it back to the other side. However, it is not necessary that the ball bounce before you hit it, except on the serve. When you hit a ball "out of the air" after the serve before it bounces it is a perfectly legal thing to do, and it is called a volley. If the ball bounces more than once on your side of the court, it is your opponent's point.

Hitting an "out" Ball

There will be times when you hit a volley out of the air that would go out if you had let the ball go without hitting it. Even so, if you hit it and your shot goes out, it is your opponent's point.

What if a Ball Hits You?

If a ball hits a player and is not returned to the other side of the net, it is a point for the other player. If a ball hits a player even though the ball would have gone out of bounds it is still a point for the other player. Even if the player is out of bounds and the ball hits them before it bounces, it is a point for the other player.

Resolving Disagreements on Whether the Ball is in or Out

It is the responsibility of the player on whose side the ball bounces to call whether it is "in" or "out." This is one of the reasons that tennis is called a game for ladies and gentlemen. It takes integrity to call a ball that is close to the line in when it means you will lose a point or even the game. A lady or a gentleman has the perspective to know that his/her integrity is more important than winning or losing a point or game.

However, there are times when you may play someone who is obviously cheating by calling balls that are unquestionably in as balls that are out. What should we do?

Most games of tennis are what we call friendly games. In other words, they are games among friends. In this event, if your friend or acquaintance is calling your "in" balls "out" at first you may overlook this as an honest mistake.

If it continues, the next time it happens you should simply ask "are you sure it was out." This gives your opponent an opportunity to "make right" the poor call. If the opponent still says the ball is out instead of in, then you must accept their call, because it is their responsibility. By asking "are you sure" it puts the other player on notice that you think they are making bad calls and often that is enough for the other player to stop making bad or questionable calls.

If your friendly opponent in the game continues to make deliberately bad calls, then you might consider playing with someone else in the future.

Overruling Your Opponent's Line Call

There is one instance when you can overrule your opponent's line call. If you hit a ball and you have a good view that your ball is out and your opponent does not have a good view and plays the ball, you should stop play and give the opponent the point.

Line Calls and School Tournaments

In the event you are playing in a school tournament, and your playing opponent is making several bad calls, then at the end of the next game, you should call a time out and ask a tournament official to make the line calls on your court.

Good Manners when Serving

When serving, you should not rush your opponent. After you are ready to serve, glance over at your opponent to see if they are ready. If they are not ready to receive the serve, give them a few extra moments to get ready.

On occasion, the server may serve and the receiver is not ready. The receiver may even try to return the serve. However, if the server notices the receiver was not ready, or the receiver tells the server he was not ready, then play the point over as a let.

The rules state that a server has 20 seconds between points to serve the next ball. This is more time than you think and is usually sufficient time for retrieving nearby balls. Of course, there are times when more time is needed to retrieve balls that have gone over the fence or rolled three or four courts over.

Since recreational players do not play with a stopwatch or clock like the professionals do, then use courtesy and common sense while keeping this rule in mind. That simply means don't take way too much time between points to rest or get a drink etc. Keep the game moving along because that is the intent of the rule.

Good Manners when Receiving

If you are receiving the serve you should try to keep up with the server's pace, but if you cannot, it is good manners to hold up your hand as a signal to the server that you are not ready yet.

If a ball rolls onto your court just before receiving a serve, you should hold up your hand calling time out to remove the ball from the court. A ball on the court can be dangerous and cause a player to turn their ankle or fall during a point.

If a ball rolls on to your court from a nearby court and needs to be removed by your opponent between the first and second serve, and it takes more than a couple of seconds to do it, the good manners thing to do is to let them start over with a first serve. Other things could happen to interrupt a server during a game and all of them cannot be listed here. Again, use good manners and if a server is interrupted during their serve, allow them to do that serve again.

A Do-Over or "let"

In tennis a do-over is called a "let." We have already mentioned that one reason to call a "let" is when the ball hits the top of the net and still goes into the service box on the serve. In this case, the server gets a do-over or "let" and serves again.

There are other times when a point can be interrupted to start a point over. One such time is when a ball rolls on to your court from a neighboring court during a point. When this happens, either player can call a let saying in a loud voice "let." The point will then start over. However, if no one calls let during the point, a let cannot be called after the point is completed.

CHAPTER 7

Different Types of Strokes in Tennis

There are six basic strokes in tennis. There is the forehand, backhand, serve, volley, overhead and lob.

The forehand is hit with the dominate hand. So, for the right-handed person, the forehand would hit balls coming to the right side of his body and balls hit to the left side would be hit as backhands. See forehand below. This is reversed for a left-hander.

See backhand below.

Serve

Every point begins with a serve. The server stands behind the baseline and serves into one of the service boxes. The server tosses the ball, and hits it above the head as the server's motion resembles a throwing motion. See below.

The Overhead

The overhead, sometimes called a smash or slam, is almost exactly like the tennis serve. A player hits an overhead after the point begins and the ball is hit back high. Because the ball is coming across the net high is why it is called an overhead because you hit it overhead like a serve.

The Volley

The volley is a shot that is hit out of the air before the ball bounces on your side. The ball is usually hit when you are close to the net. See below.

The Lob

The lob is usually a shot you hit when your opponent gets close to the net, and you want to hit it over his head. This is a good shot for slowing down a point. See below.

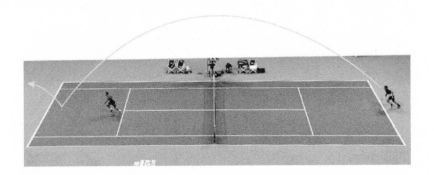

CHAPTER 8

Drills For Home

Private and group lessons are important, but you should also work on your tennis at home. Here are some good drills for beginners. These drills get progressively more difficult. Do them over and over until you can master them.

You can do most of these drills alone, but some will require a partner or parent.

Drill Set # 1

1. Standing four feet apart toss the ball underhand and catch on the first bounce with two hands. After each catch back up a step and toss again. Keep tossing and catching from the same spot until both catch and then back up another step. Repeat.

2. Same drill, but now catch with only the right hand.

3. Same drill, but now catch with the left hand.

4. Same drill but now catch without a bounce.

Drill Set # 2

1. Standing ten feet apart turn sideways, point at your target and throw overhand to your partner. Then catch your partner's throw. Continue till each catch 100 times.

2. Try to catch and throw 3 in a row. Then 5 Then 7 and work up to 10.

Drill Set # 3

1. Stand 15-20 feet away from your partner. Stand sideways and throw a tennis ball overhand to your partner without them having to take more than one step in any direction to catch the ball. (Overhand as opposed to side-arm - Google Quarterback throwing motion if you need an example). Throw the ball at a speed that can be easily caught (not too fast or hard). The assignment is complete when you can throw 100 of these in a row. The throwing motion is the motion used when serving a tennis ball.

2. Balance a tennis ball on the face of the racquet while holding the racquet with only one hand with fingers up (as opposed to the back of the hand up). Roll the ball around the outer edge of the racquet without letting the ball fall off. The assignment

is complete when the student can circle the outer edge ten times without the ball falling off. Then have the ball go in the opposite direction.

3. Self-rally starts by tossing the ball up and after the bounce hit the ball up a 2-3 feet, let the ball bounce on the ground and hit it up again. The assignment is complete when a student can self-rally the ball 100 times without a miss.

Drill Set # 4

1. Same as exercise 1 in Homework Assignment # 3, except move back to 30 feet.

2. Bounce the ball up from the strings of your racquet without it bouncing on the ground like the old paddle ball game. Student should grip the racquet with fingers up. Assignment is complete when student can bounce the ball 40 times without a miss.

3. Repeat #2 but while gripping with the fingers facing down.

Drill Set # 5

1. Warm up with 10-20 overhand throws from 30 feet. Then throw the ball 10 times as far as you can. Take the three longest

throws and average them. This drill is to help you improve your throwing power. Do this drill on different days to measure your improvements on distance after your first tries on the first day. Chart your progress.

2. Dribble a tennis ball with your racquet. Racquet grip is with fingers down. Assignment is complete when student can dribble 50 times without a miss.

Drill Set # 6

1. Dribble tennis ball while moving from one end of a hard, flat surface to the other like a tennis court, driveway or gym floor. The assignment is complete when the student can dribble 50 times without a miss.

2. Stroke the ball against a wall. Use a red practice ball and stand 7 - 9 feet away from the wall. Hit softly 7 - 10 feet up on the wall allowing the ball to bounce three to six feet from the wall where you will hit it again. The assignment is complete when you can hit fifty balls in a row without a miss. After you can do this with a red ball, go to the orange ball, then the green dot ball and eventually the yellow ball.

Section I Review Questions

1. Correct score keeping is: ___, 15, 30, ____, ____

2. What does the word love mean in tennis?

3. At the beginning of a new game, who is required to call out the set score?

4. Before each serve, the server calls out what?

5. Before the server begins to serve, he/she should have at least two _____.

6. If the ball lands on the line, it is out. T or F

7. If your opponent hits a winner and his/her foot touches the bottom of the net whose point is it?

8. The harder you work at your tennis game, the better you will get. T or F

9. To master the game of tennis could take many years. T or F

10. If your opponent wasn't sure if your shot was in or out what should happen?

11. If you are 8 feet behind the service line and your opponent hits a ball so far out of the court that it is going to hit the back fence and you catch the ball before it lands whose point is it?

12. When your serve clips the net and lands in the service box it is called a let and you get to serve that serve over. If it happens again on the next serve do you still get to serve again? Yes or No

13. When you are receiving a serve, the ball must bounce in the service box before you hit the ball. T or F

14. The person receiving the serve must stand inside the service box. T or F

15. How many service boxes are on a tennis court?

16. How many times is the ball allowed to bounce on your side of the court?

17. How do you determine who serves first in a match?

18. While serving, if the ball hits the net and falls in your opponent's service box the serve is considered a let and the server gets another serve. T or F.

19. Whose responsibility is it to call the ball in or out on your opponent's side of the court?

20. If your opponent calls several balls out that you clearly see in what should you say?

21. You switch sides of the court on odd or even games?

22. Missing both first and second serves is called a double fault. T or F

23. After the first game players switch sides of the court? T or F

24. Players continue to switch side on odd numbered games throughout the set. T or F

25. Becoming a good tennis player takes a love for the game and a dedication to learning it over a several year span of time. T or F

26. Becoming a good tennis player takes commitment to practice and learning the intricacies and subtleties of the game. T or F

27. When the ball is out on your side of the court, you should call it out immediately without hesitation. T or F

28. Your opponent hits a serve that you call out but your opponent thinks it was good. Whose call is it?

29. How many times is the server allowed to toss the ball during the serve without hitting it?

30. The server has _____ chances to hit a good serve in the proper service box.

31. The server should not serve until the receiver is ready? True of False

32. The doubles alley refers to the area between the singles sideline and doubles sideline? T or F

33. If the score is 40/30 and the receiver wins the point. What will the score be?

34. You must serve into the advantage court during odd numbered points like 30/15.

35. A "let" that happens once a point begins means that you play the point over? Yes or No

36. Correct scorekeeping order is:

a.   45, 35, 20, 10

b.   Love, 15, 30, 40, Game

c.   15, 30, 45, love

d.   15, 30, 40, love

37. The player who serves the ball to start the points is called the _____.

38. If the ball lands on the line, it is out. T or F

39. Playing tennis helps improve a. eye hand coordination, b. endurance, c. foot quickness. Is the answer a. b. c. or all the above?

40. The service box is an area on the court that the person must stand in to receive a serve. T or F

41. Missing the first and second serve is called a deuce. T or F

42. In tennis love means "I just won, but I still want to be your friend. T or F

43. The ball can bounce twice on each side of the net. T or F

44. The server gets two attempts to make a good serve. T or F

45. If I'm serving and I win the first 2 points of the game, what is the score?

46. List three parts of a tennis racquet.

47. When the ball goes back and forth during a game is that called a volley or a rally. T or F

48. Before each serve, the server calls out the score. T or F

49. The game of tennis can be played with 2 to 4 players. True or False.

50. In a serve, the ball must hit the ground before the receiving side may hit it. T or F

51. In tennis, only the receiving side can score. T or F

52. The server delivers the ball from behind the baseline. T or F

53. How do you begin the game of tennis? a. run a mile b. spin the racquet c. whoever wants to go first.

54. In tennis, either the serving or receiving side may score. True or False

55. The ready or waiting position is the best position to get in before receiving the ball. T or F

56. You must begin the game by serving into the deuce court. True or False

57. If a ball lands on the line it is in play? T or F

58. Name two types of strokes in tennis:

59. In the ready position, your feet should be pointing at the right sideline. T or F

60. The boundary lines that run from the net to the baseline are called the service line. T or F

61. Failure on an attempt to serve into the proper court is called a let. T or F

SECTION II

CHAPTER 9

Improving is Fun

The game of tennis is a lot of fun, but it is a challenging game to master and can take many years to become a good player. The longer you play and the more you learn about how to play, the more you will grow as a player. The more you learn about the game and how to play it, the more fun it becomes.

Unlike a lot of other games, tennis is a game that you can play for the rest of your life. If you practice and learn the game while you are young, you will always have people who will want to play with you or have you on their team. Tennis is a good game for making friends and learning how to win and lose with class and be a good sport. Tennis is a lot like life and the more you play the game, the more you learn about life and yourself.

Everyone likes to win, but since tennis is a game that you will play for a long time, you will have your share of wins and losses. Every opportunity you have to play a different person, you will learn that different people offer different challenges on how to play the game. No two people will play the game exactly alike. So, if you lose today to someone, you can learn from that experience and it helps you become a better, and more well-rounded player for the future. You may even use losing a match as an opportunity to learn and improve. With tennis, there is always a chance to improve or even win the next time you play.

Most every experienced tennis players will tell you the way to improve faster is to play someone a little better than you. Each time you do, it makes you a bit better too. So, if you always win, that may mean that you need to play someone who is better than you so that you can learn and become an even better player. Winning a tennis match doesn't make you a winner, and neither does losing a tennis match make you a loser.

Whether you win or lose, you try to become a little better player with each match. In tennis, one day you may win a match against a person, and the next day you may lose to the same person. Some days you play better, and other days your competition plays better. It is the same way in life. A tennis player who wants to keep getting better looks for opportunities to play someone who is a better player. Like the old proverb says, "As iron sharpens iron, so one man sharpens another." Playing a better person makes you sharper.

Often in the same game, tennis has ebbs and flows, ups and downs, high points and low points and shifts in momentum. You should never get overconfident if you are winning or disappointed when you are losing because the momentum can change fast. One game you may be playing better than your competition and the next game your competition may be playing better than you. So, it is vital whether you are ahead or behind, that you play every point in every game the best you can. That is how you show respect for yourself and your competition.

In tennis, the real definition of a winner is the one who keeps playing their best regardless of being ahead or behind. In school, fighting is a bad thing, but being a fighter on the tennis court is a compliment because it means that you always do your best regardless of the score. If you play like that, you will gain a reputation as a player who is a strong fighter.

CHAPTER 10

More Important than Winning

Like I said before, everyone likes to win, but there are several things more important than winning in tennis. Let's look at a few of the more important things.

1. **Learning the game.** The more you play, the more you learn about your own game and how others play. Learning the game is more important than winning.

2. **Improving as a player.** Like we said before, you improve faster if you play people who are better than you. So, it is better to play more skilled players than to win.

3. **Gaining competitive experience.** The more competitive experience you gain, the better you become as a player. Just hitting the ball around with friends in a non-competitive way is fun, but doesn't usually make you a better player. Playing in a tournament or other competitive matches will make you better. Playing in competitive matches is more important than winning.

4. **Your integrity, your reputation and your relationship with other players** is more important than winning. Some kids want to win too badly. Wanting to win too much can cause them to do several things that will cause a bad reputation and hurt their relationships with other kids. Things, like getting too angry and cursing or acting out in other ways, damage your reputation. Some kids even cheat by calling balls out that are in. No one likes playing with a kid like this. So, playing fair, keeping your composure and having fun in a match is more important than winning.

CHAPTER 11

Playing the Percentages

Crosscourt and Down-the-Line

Now is time to introduce a new term. The term is crosscourt. When you are standing on the left side of the court and hit the ball on the other side of the center line, you have hit the ball crosscourt. See photo below: Same is true if you are standing on the right side of the court and hit it over the centerline to the left side.

The above photo is an example of a crosscourt shot.

Here is another term. Down-the-line. A down-the-line shot is when you are standing on one side of the court either left or right and hit the ball without crossing over the center line. See diagram below.

Above is an example of hitting a shot down the line.

Position on the Court

Where to stand on the court often depends on the location where your competitor is standing when He returns the ball. Generally speaking, the ideal place to stand is just behind the baseline in the middle or center of the court.

During a point, you will need to run to different parts of the court to hit the ball. Once you return the ball, you will need to reposition yourself for your competitors next shot. This repositioning is called "**recovery**" and is usually moving back to the center of the court to get ready for your competitor's next shot.

One of the first footwork moves you should learn in tennis is known as the split-step. The split-step is used when the player is preparing herself to move to the next ball but isn't sure where the next shot is going. The split-step is essentially a bounce step where the player bounces into the ready position mentioned earlier, and this prepares the player to move in all directions. We will go over the split-step in more detail later.

Playing Smart High Percentage Tennis

Which is the safest and better shot to hit "Crosscourt" or "Down-the-Line? Now it is time to remember the court dimensions of a tennis court. A tennis court is 78 feet from baseline to baseline. See below.

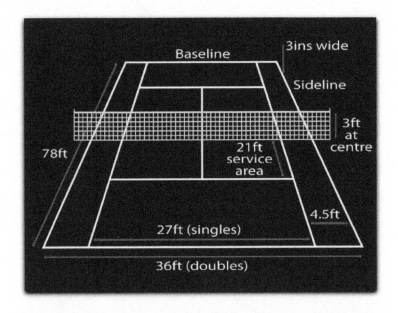

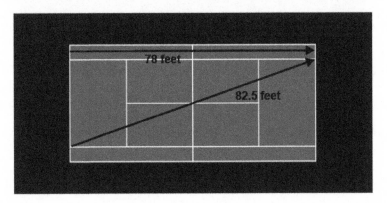

This diagram shows that the court is 82.5 feet diagonally from one corner to the other.

What this means is that you have 4.5 feet more space for your ball to go into the court when you hit crosscourt verses down-the-line, so that means that going crosscourt is the safer or higher percentage shot.

Also, remember the dimensions of the net. See below.

The net is 3 feet high in the middle at the net strap and 3.5 feet high at the net posts. So, hitting the ball crosscourt means that you have six fewer inches to get over the net. This also makes hitting the ball crosscourt a safer and higher percentage shot.

Understanding Your Competitors Highest Percentage Shot

It is also important to anticipate where your opponent may hit his next shot. If you send your shot deep and crosscourt the highest percentage shot for your opponent is also to send it back crosscourt. Though he may send the ball down-the-line, there is a good chance he/she will send it right back crosscourt to you since that is the safest shot.

Also, knowing the most likely place where your competitor is hitting the ball will affect where you go to position yourself for the next shot. Instead of going all the way to the middle of the court on the baseline, the best place is to recover is almost back to middle, but shade a little to the side you expect them to hit the ball. So, if you are on the right side of the court and hit crosscourt and deep, then go almost back to the middle but stay on the right side of the center. See the image below.

The Lob

A high and deep looping shot back to your opponent is called a lob. This can be a perfect shot, especially when your competitor hits a shot deep that backs you up far behind the baseline. Hitting a high lob can give you time to recover back to a good position on the court and ready for their next shot.

Hitting the Ball with Spin

The tennis ball is always spinning or rotating with each shot. One of the ways that players learn to control the ball is with spin. There are two main types of spin; top-spin and under-spin also called slice. If you hit the ball and it is spinning away from you, it is top-spin and if you hit the ball and it is spinning back toward you, the spin is underspin or slice.

Top Spin

Two good things happen when you hit the ball with topspin. The first is that it lifts the ball so it will be high enough to get over the net. Second, the spinning ball causes the air around it to force the ball back down into the court and keeps it from going too far and out of bounds.

To hit the ball with topspin the player must start the racquet out low and swing the racquet on an upward path. This swing path makes the ball spin away from the player with top-spin. See the example below.

Underspin or slice

Sometimes a player wants to hit the ball with underspin. An underspin shot has several names. It is mostly called a slice but is also called a chip shot, a drop shot and a chop shot. The volley is usually hit with underspin too.

Two good things happen when you hit the ball with slice. The first is that it keeps the ball lower and this is a good thing especially when you are close to the net and trying to make sure you don't hit the ball too far and out of bounds. Secondly, when the ball bounces, it stays lower to the ground than a ball hit with topspin and gives your opponent less time to get to the ball and hit it. Underspin is also used a lot when a player is running for a wide shot and just trying to get it back in play.

Hitting the ball with slice is almost the exact opposite of hitting it with topspin. The player must start the racquet out high and swing the racquet on a downward path. This makes the ball spin back toward the player who hit it. The following is an example of hitting with slice.

Strategies

Because there are many different types of shots, there are many different strategies that players use to win a point. They may stay back at the baseline and hit high looping topspin shots that bounce high to their opponent, or they may hit low backspin shots that rush their opponent. The longer you play and practice you will discover a lot of different strategies you can use to win a point. Often the best players will mix up strategies to keep their opponent off balance.

CHAPTER 12

The Tennis Grips

Continental Tennis Grip

Different strokes or shots are hit using different grips. The Continental grip is the most used grip. It is used for the serve, the forehand, backhand, the volley and for the forehand and backhand slice. To demonstrate these grips, we will need to revisit the racquet handle. See below the grip is positioned with the racquet on its edge.

The next reference point for being able to demonstrate the grip is the dominate hand. We will demonstrate with the right hand as being the dominant hand.

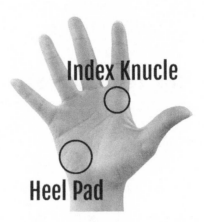

Notice the circles on the index knuckle and the heel pad. For a continental grip, the index knuckle and heel pad should both be placed on position 2 of the racquet. See Continental grip below.

The Continental grip is the standard for serves and overheads, as it allows you to bend the wrist inward after the shot naturally. It is also the preferred grip for volleys, making an open face easier on both the forehand and backhand side. It is also good for quick forehand and backhand volleys because it does not require a grip change. It is also best for forehand and backhand slice shots making underspin easier.

The disadvantage of the continental grip is that it is more difficult to hit topspin on the ball.

Eastern Forehand Grip

The eastern tennis grip is used mainly for forehands as is the semi-western grip. Both grips are popular for hitting forehands among players, but the semi-western gives the ball a little more topspin. On the Eastern forehand, the index knuckle and heel pad are placed on the 3 position on the racquet as seen below.

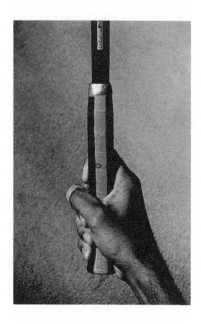

The Advantages and Disadvantages of an Eastern Forehand

The Eastern forehand is one of the easiest forehand grips to learn. Most beginners start out with this grip, but pros also use it. The advantages of this grip are that it is easy to change from it to the continental grip which many players often do. Many players will serve with the Continental grip, hit their first forehand with an eastern forehand and then finish the point at the net with a volley using the continental grip again. Players can also get more topspin on their shots using an eastern forehand over a continental.

The disadvantages of the eastern forehand grip are it is more difficult to control high balls in your upper strike zone.

The Semi-western Forehand

On the semi-western forehand, the index knuckle and heel pad are placed on the number 4 position on the racquet. See below.

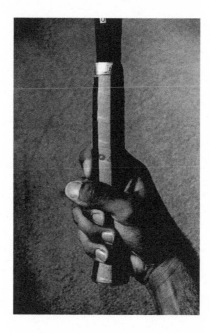

Advantage and Disadvantages of the Semi-western Forehand

The Semi-western forehand grip provides both topspin control and power. It is easier to hit higher balls in your upper strike zones.

The disadvantage of the Semi-western forehand grip is that low balls are more difficult to hit. It is also a more challenging grip change between it and the continental grip.

Two-handed Backhand Grip

For this discussion, we will only describe the two-handed backhand since it is easier to learn than the one-handed backhand. Once you learn the two-handed backhand, it will make the one-handed backhand easier to use if you decide to learn it. Most professional players today use the two-hand backhand grip, though some of the top players use the one-handed.

There is more than one way to grip the two-handed backhand, however, we will only demonstrate the one we feel is the best one to learn first.

For right-hander's, grip with the right hand just as you would for the continental grip. Slide the left hand on top and put it in the left-handed Eastern forehand. See below.

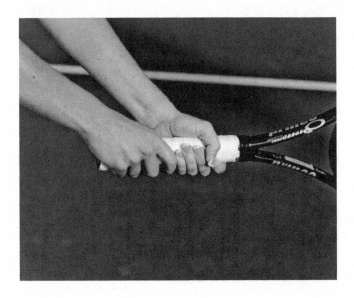

CHAPTER 13

Consistency is the Number One Strategy

Hitting the Ball with Consistency

Hitting the ball with power can give a player an advantage over the player who does not hit with power. However, it is usually the player who hits with the most control and consistency that has the true advantage.

The number one strategy in tennis is to hit the ball back across the net one more time than your opponent on each point. If you can do this, you will win every point. Playing with consistency is harder than it sounds for two reasons. First, controlling a tennis balls direction, speed, spin and trajectory is not easy. Secondly, your tennis opponent is hitting the ball in all types of different ways during a match. Seldom do you receive two balls from your opponent that are the same.

Because the balls come with such a variety of spins, speeds and trajectories, it is difficult to hit the ball with consistency. It takes lots of practice. The number one way that a player learns to control the ball is with spin. Hitting the ball with topspin causes the ball to first clear the net and then to dip down and into the court.

Hitting the ball with Power and Speed

Once a player has learned to control the tennis ball and comes more consistent, then he or she will want to learn to hit the ball with more power and speed. However, learning to hit with consistency first is important because that allows you to hit with more power without losing control of the ball. It does a player little good to hit a ball hard and fast if they are not able to keep the ball in the court.

Hitting the ball faster and with more power means the racquet head is moving faster. The number one tool to use for making the racquet head move faster is the ground. That may sound unusual at first, but it is true.

How Does the Ground Help You Hit the Ball with Power?

First of all, you must remember that the ground is the platform you are standing on. Think of a baseball pitcher. During his wind up, he uses the ground to spring forward and toward home plate as he delivers the ball as fast as he can.

In the same way, the ground is a springboard for transferring your weight into the ball sending it to the other side of the court. There are several tennis strokes or shots that use the ground to either step into or spring into.

When hitting the serve the player bends their knees and springs into the ball. With both backhand and forehand players either spring into or step into these shots. Also, the volley is a shot where the player steps or springs into the shot. And of course, the ground is where we find our balance and what we push off of when we change directions.

Section I Review Questions

1. You often learn more about how to be a better tennis player by losing a match? T or F

2. Winning a tennis match makes you a winner and losing a match makes you a loser. T or F

3. Tennis is a game of ebbs and flows, ups and downs, high points and low points and shifts in momentum. How should you play when you get ahead in a match? Why?

4. The real definition of a winner is the one who keeps playing their best and fighting back regardless of being ahead or behind. T or F

5. How should you play when you get behind in a match? Why?

6. When you play tennis competitively, you learn things about yourself. T or F

7. Playing mentally tough tennis is when you learn to play every point competitively and with intensity whether ahead or behind. T or F

8. Letting up when you get ahead in a match is a sign of having a poor understanding of the ebbs and flows and momentum of tennis. T or F

9. Becoming discouraged when you get behind in a match is a sign of having a poor understanding of the ebbs and flows and momentum of tennis. T or F

10. Real growth in tennis comes when we are challenged to improve by someone who is better than us. A real competitor looks for opportunities to play someone better than himself. T or F

11. We never get better if we only want to play people we know we can beat. T or F

12. What is more important than winning? Circle all that you believe are true to you.

    a) Your integrity (Doing what is right as opposed to cheating)

    b) Your reputation as a player among friends and other players

    c) Your relationship with competitors as a tough yet honest player

    d) Learning the game

    e) Improving as a player

    f) Gaining competitive experience

    g) All of the above.

13. The shot that gives you highest percentage chances of getting the ball in is the crosscourt shot. Why? (hint: two reasons)

14. When you hit the ball crosscourt to your opponent, what is his safest shot to hit back to you, crosscourt or down the line?

15. Where should you recover to after you hit a ball crosscourt?

16. When your opponent pushes you deep beyond the baseline with little time to recover or use the shot you like, what is often a good shot to choose to give you more time and get you back in the point?

17. There are many different strategies to winning a tennis match? T or F

18. The chip shot has what type of spin?

19. Kids who are polite, play fair, and handle losing well are called

    a) a. sore losers

    b) b. braggers

    c) c. good sports

20. Your team just lost the last soccer game of the season. What would a good sport do?

    a) Yell at your teammates for doing a bad job.

    b) Shake hands and congratulate the winning team.

c) Say mean things to the winning team.

21. Let balls only occur on the serve. T or F

22. If on the serve the receiver is not ready but makes an attempt to return the ball and fails, the receiver loses the point. T or F Explain.

23. You hit a ball down the sideline that you see clearly out on your opponent's side. Your opponent is running to get the ball and can't tell whether the ball was in or out and plays the ball. What should happen?

    a) You continue to play the point since your opponent didn't say anything.

    b) You move to the net to put away the ball since your opponent made a weak return because they could barely get to the ball.

    c) You stop play and call a let to play the point over.

    d) You tell your opponent that your ball was out and you lose the point.

24. What is called during the point if a ball rolls on a court or a distraction from someone beside the player on the court?

    a) life

b) love

c) let

d) Log

25. An overhead is also called a

    a) slash

    b) mudpuppy

    c) kill

    d) Smash

26. If a player is standing anywhere outside the court and the ball hits the player before it bounces, what is the result.

    a) The player who hit the ball loses the point.

    b) The player whom the ball hit, loses the point.

    c) The point is replayed because no one is sure where the ball was going to bounce.

27. You accidentally touch the net during a point. You're running to get to a ball and you get it just as it bounces a second time. You lose the point in both instances. Who must make the call (decides the outcome), you or your opponent? Assume there is no referee or umpire around.

a) you

b) your opponent

28. If the score is 30 all, the server should be serving to the deuce court. T or F

29. If the ball is in bounds a player can go out of bounds to return it. T or F

30. If a ball from another court rolls along the baseline of your opponent's court and your opponents are not disturbed by the ball because they do not see it, are you allowed to call a let and why?

31. A volley usually hit with underspin. Tor F

32. The best volley grip is a continental grip. T or F

33. The eastern forehand grip has the index knuckle and heel of the hand on the number three position? T or F

34. No Ad scoring refers to a scoring system that when the score reaches 40/40 the next player to win a point wins the game. T or F

35. In add scoring, a player wins the game if after the game reaches 40/40 he or she wins the next two point. T or F

36. One of the most important weapons a player has to use against his opponent is the ground because...

    a) He can use the ground to spring into his serve.

    b) He can use the ground as a platform to jump into his forehand and backhand.

    c) He can use the ground to step to on his volleys.

    d) He can use the ground for balance and change of direction for split step.

    e) All of the above.

37. A "Tie-breaker" is played when both players are tied at six games each? T or F

38. If your opponent hits a first serve and the ball hits you in the leg before it even bounces, whose point is it?

39. Your opponent hits a ball that is obviously out and you call it out, but catch it before it hits the ground to keep from having to run after it. My opponent called it his point. Is he correct? Yes or No

40. How much time do you have between games when you switch sides of the court?

41. The player who serves first in a tie-breaker of a singles match, shall be the player who received in the last game of the set. T or F

42. Can the receiver of serve disrupt the server's routine to clear a ball that has bounced onto the playing area? Yes or No

43. The split step helps you to be ready to go either left or right? True or False

44. If the server is interrupted during the delivery of the second serve, how many serves is the server entitled to?

45. Your opponent volleys a ball before it crosses the net. Whose point is it?

46. Juniors often play what is called pro sets to speed up the tournament. How many games are in a pro set?

47. Juniors often play no-ad scoring. "No add" scoring is when the score is 40/40 and the next person who wins a point, wins the game? T or F

48. When the ball is in play, another ball rolls onto the court, a let is called. The server had previously served a fault on his first serve. Is the server now entitled to a first serve or second serve?

49. The racquet handle has eight bevels when you look at the butt of the racquet. T or F

50. The reference point for gripping the racquet are racquet bevels, the index knuckle and the heel of the hand. T or F

51. Hitting the ball with spin makes it harder to control the tennis ball. T or F

52. Consistently getting the ball back over the net and into the court should be the number one strategy for every beginning tennis player. T or F

53. The two-handed backhand is more difficult to learn than the one handed backhand and the pro players all use a one-handed backhand. T or F

54. What is the advantages and disadvantages of the continental grip?

55. What are the advantages and disadvantages of the Eastern Forehand grip?

56. What are the advantages and disadvantages of the Semi-Western grip?

57. The Semi-Western grip has the index knuckle and the heel of the hand on the third bevel. T or F

58. To begin counting the bevels on the tennis racquet, the number one position is on top. However, to find the top does the racquet need to be laying on its side or on its edge?

59. A topspin shot rotates away from the person who hit it. True or False

60. Name two grips used in tennis.

SECTION III

CHAPTER 14

The Armband Color Levels

Kaizen Tennis mimics the karate martial arts belt system, using colored armbands to mark levels of improvements and competencies. Below are the competencies for the first five levels. Ultimately, ten levels end in the black arm band.

Competencies and the Arm Band System

Level 1 - White – Beginner

Level 2 - Pink

Level 2 - Pink Footwork

1. Can assume the athletic ready position

2. Can perform a split step.

3. Uses feet to demonstrate shoulder turn on forehand and backhand.

4. Can run and stop quickly.

5. Can change speed and direction.

6. Can shuffle and gallop.

7. Can walk backward and on balance.

8. Can jump line 5 times.

Level 2 - Pink Hands and Racquet

1. Knows how to hold racquet while in the ready position.

2. Tosses and catches ball with either hand on the bounce high, low, deep, short with a partner.

3. Toss ball with either hand to a target.

4. Throw overhand into deuce court from service line.

5. Can catch a ball on the face of the racquet 5 out of 10 times.

Level 2 - Pink Forehand/Backhand

1. Can self-rally on forehand and backhand consecutively 10 times

2. Can rally with partner over a line.

3. Drop hit to multiple targets with forehand and backhand.

4. Hits ball tossed by partner left/right/center with forehand and backhand.

5. Can demonstrate a low to high swing path on forehand and backhand in slow motion.

Level 2 - Pink Serve and Return

1. Can serve underhand with drop serve 5 out of 10 times into the deuce court.

2. Can serve 5 out of 10 over-hand with sideways stance and safe serve position from inside the service line.

3. **Return:** Can move their weight side to side when server tosses to serve.

4. Can return 3 out of 10 second serves across the net.

Level 2 - Pink Overhead

1. Player can get in the overhead stance and move up, back and side to side.

2. Can catch 3 of 10 balls in their off hand on the bounce.

3. Can hit 3 of 10 overheads with their the racquet face on the bounce.

Level 2 - Pink Volley

1. Steps across and blocks the ball.

2. Volleys with racquet head above wrist.

3. Can hit forehand volley left, right and center with coach toss.

Level 2 - Pink Lob

1. Can drop feed 3 out of 10 from the service line and hit over the coach standing at the net.

Level 2 - Pink Game Understanding

2. Knows the scoring progression.

3. Knows all the parts to a racquet.

4. Knows how to call balls in and out.

5. Knows where to stand on serve and return.

6. Understands the basics of a forehand and a backhand grip.

7. Understands where to serve.

Level 2 - Pink Character Development

1. Introduced to Kaizen concept that improving is fun.

2. Improvement requires more practice at home.

3. Respects coach and other players and equipment.

4. Listens and follows instructions.

5. Shows gratitude by saying thank you.

Level 3 - Green

Level 3 - Green Footwork

1. Steps out on unit turn.

2. Moves to get beside the ball prior to stroke.

3. Can split step and push off to the right and left.

4. Understands recovery.

5. Can move backward quickly on balance.

6. Pivot forward and back.

7. Hop on 1 leg across the court.

8. 25 jump ropes in a row.

Level 3 - Green Hands and Racquet

1. Toss ball with either hand to all 4 quadrants from three feet behind the net on the center line.

2. Can shuffle and catch from baseline to net and back. (two misses)

3. Can throw overhand throw into service boxes from halfway between service line and baseline. (Court adjusted for age)

4. Performs unit turn with racquet up and in position on forehand and backhand.

Level 3 - Green Forehand/Backhand

1. Uses eastern forehand grip on forehands.

2. Uses a two-handed backhand with dominant hand at continental to eastern and off-hand at eastern.

3. Can demonstrate in slow motion how to rotate trunk on forehand and backhand with controlled follow through.

4. Can self-rally alternating sides of the racquet 50 times in a row.

5. Rallies over net with partner from service line.

6. Can hit a self-fed ball into the 4 quadrants of the court 3 out of 10 times from the T with both forehand and backhand.

7. Can hit 5 out of 10 forehand and backhand groundstrokes fed by coach back in play.

Level 3 - Green Serve and Return

1. Serve to opponents forehand and backhand 3 out of 10 times from the service line while using the Continental to Eastern forehand grip from the service line using the safe serve position.

2. Can serve 5 out of 10 from midway between service line and baseline using the Continental to Eastern Forehand grip with a safe serve stance.

3. Can demonstrate a safe serve in slow motion.

4. **Return:** Can return 3 of 10 second serves beyond the service line.

Level 3 - Green Overhead

1. Player can demonstrate overhead in slow motion.

2. Player uses continental to eastern forehand grip while hitting overhead.

3. Player can catch 7 of 10 balls with off hand on the bounce.

4. Player can hit 5 of 10 balls off the bounce from inside the service line.

Level 3 - Green Volley

1. Use Continental to eastern forehand grip on forehand and backhand volleys.

2. Can demonstrate forehand volley stepping diagonally, the knee bend, opening the face for a volley, racquet head above the

wrist, keeping head and racquet head close to same height, with contact point in front.

3. Can hit 5 out of 10 coach fed forehand volleys back in play from 3 feet behind the net.

4. Approach and volley - Can drop feed an approach shot, come forward, split step and hit 5 out of 10 volleys from 3 feet behind net.

5. Can forehand volley 3 out of 10 short inside the service line.

6. Can forehand volley 3 out of 10 deep beyond the service line.

7. Can one-handed backhand volley 3 out of 10 coach tossed volleys.

Level 3 - Green Lob

1. Can demonstrate the defensive forehand lob in slow motion.

2. Can drop feed 5 out of 10 forehand lobs from the service line and hit over the coach standing at the net.

3. Can drop feed 3 out of 10 backhand lobs from the service line and hit over the coach standing at the net.

4. Can hit 3 out of 10 coach fed defensive forehand lobs over the coach standing at the net.

Level 3 - Green Game Understanding

1. Understands all the rules of the game and can answer questions under section 1 of this book with 85% accuracy.

Level 3 - Green Character Development

1. Realizes that moving from one level to the next is fun.

2. Knows improvement takes practicing when no one is watching.

3. Compliments partners and teammates.

4. Acts with kindness toward others.

5. Shakes hands after match.

Level 4 - Red

Level 4 - Red Footwork

1. Can do drop-step then cross-over with shuffle.

2. Can Carioca.

3. Can sideway skip.

4. Can hop on either foot from doubles sideline to doubles sideline.

5. Returns to ready position after serve.

6. Recovers off center based where shot is hit.

7. Hits forehand with open and semi-open stance.

8. Can make shuffle adjustment steps to hit with an open stance.

Level 4 - Red Hands and Racquet

1. Can catch ball tossed the length of the doubles alley in either hand out of the air 8 of 10 times.

2. Can shuffle and catch with partner with either hand from baseline to net and back. (two misses).

3. Can throw into either service box from baseline (Court adjusted for age).

4. Can do 10 paddle ball rallies with forehand and backhand.

5. Can dribble the ball 10 times in a row.

Level 4 - Red Forehand/Backhand

1. Can demonstrate a continental, eastern and semi-western forehand grip.

2. Can demonstrate the forehand and backhand stroke in slow motion.

3. Can demonstrate big C and little C on forehand and backhand in slow motion.

4. Can demonstrate how to put topspin on both the forehand and backhand.

5. Nondominant hand on throat of racquet on the takeback.

6. Gets good spacing between themselves and the ball.

7. Rallies crosscourt, down the line, and side to side with partner.

8. Can hit a self-fed ball into the 4 quadrants of the court 5 out of 10 times from the T with both forehand and backhand.

9. Can hit 5 out of 10 forehand and backhand groundstrokes fed by coach back in play.

10. Can hit 3 out of 10 forehands and backhands coach feed crosscourt and down the line.

11. Can hit 3 out of 10 slice backhands and forehands in play from the service line.

Level 4 - Red Serve and Return

1. Serve to opponents forehand and backhand 3 out of 10 times from the baseline line to both deuce and add court using the safe serve position.

2. Serve 3 out of 10 serves from the baseline using a Continental to Eastern forehand grip while using a pro service motion.

3. Can perform 7 of 10 safe serves from baseline using a safe serve stance. Serve demonstrates a knee bend with toss.

4. Player can demonstrate an ideal trophy pose.

5. **Return:** Moves into court on server's toss, split steps and moves to ball.

6. Returns 5 of 10 second serves beyond the service line.

Level 4 - Red Overhead

1. Player uses continental grip while hitting overhead.

2. Player can catch 5 of 10 balls with off-hand out of the air.

3. Player can hit 7 out of 10 overheads off the bounce

4. Player can hit 3 of 10 out of the air into play.

5. Player can hit 3 out of 10 overheads off the bounce down the line.

6. Player can hit 3 out of 10 overheads off the bounce cross court.

Level 4 - Red Volley

1. Uses continental grip on forehand and backhand volleys.

2. Can demonstrate both forehand and backhand volley technique in slow motion.

3. Can hit 5 out of 10 forehand volleys from 5 feet behind the net.

4. Can hit 5 out of 10 coach fed approach shots down the line and finish with a forehand putaway volley while completing 2 split steps.

5. Can forehand volley 5 out of 10 short inside the service line.

6. Can forehand volley 5 out of 10 deep beyond the service line.

7. Can one-handed backhand volley 5 out of 10 coach fed volleys.

8. Can hit 3 out of 10 catch volleys that are below the net.

9. Can hit 3 out of 10 high volleys hitting down with power.

10. Can hit 3 out of 10 forehand volleys crosscourt.

11. Can hit 3 out of 10 forehand volleys down the line.

Level 4 - Red Lob

1. Can demonstrate the defensive backhand lob is slow motion.

2. Can drop feed 7 out of 10 forehand lobs from the baseline and hit over the coach standing between net and service line.

3. Can drop feed 5 out of 10 backhand lobs from the baseline and hit over the coach standing between net and service line.

4. Can hit 5 out of 10 coaches feed defensive forehand lobs over the coach standing at the net.

5. Can hit 3 out of 10 coaches feed defensive backhand lobs over the coach standing at the net.

6. Can hit 3 out of 10 coach feed offensive forehand lobs over the coach standing at the net.

Level 4 - Red Game Understanding

1. Remembers score and announces it while serving.

2. Keeps set score with the net-post scorekeeper.

3. Can answer questions under section 2 of this book with 85% accuracy.

Level 4 - Red Character Development

1. Beginning to realize how improving their skills makes playing more fun.

2. Shifting from a focus on winning to focusing on improvement.

3. Begins to see losing a match as an opportunity to improve.

4. Gives opponent the benefit of the doubt on close line calls.

5. Puts others above self.

Level 5 - Orange

Level 5 - Orange Footwork

1. Can perform crossover step on wide balls.

2. Open/semi-open stance on high and wide balls.

3. Can cross over and do gallop shuffle step when moving for a short ball.

4. Drop step-crossover-shuffle when backing up.

5. Can skip backward.

6. Can line jump side to side and forward and back on balance on either foot 10 times.

Level 5 - Orange Hands and Racquet

1. Is changing grips quickly from forehand to Continental grip to hit volleys.

2. Can do 25 paddle ball rallies with forehand and backhand.

3. Can paddleball 10 times in a row alternating between forehand and backhand.

4. Can dribble 25 times in a row.

Level 5 - Orange Forehand/Backhand

1. Can demonstrate a slice forehand and backhand in slow motion.

2. Can hit a self-fed ball into the 4 quadrants of the court 7 out of 10 times from the T with both forehand and backhand.

3. Can hit 7 out of 10 forehand and backhand groundstrokes fed by coach back in play.

4. Can hit 5 out of 10 forehands and backhands coach feed crosscourt and down the line.

5. Can hit 5 out of 10 slice backhands and forehands in play from inside the baseline.

6. Can hit 3 out of 10 heavy topspin forehands with at least 10 feet net clearance with a semi-western grip.

7. Can rally with a partner from the service line using only slice.

8. Can rally consistently hitting the ball at least to mid court with good height over the net.

9. Can hit coach hand fed ball into the 4 quadrants of the court 3 out of 10 times from the baseline with forehand and backhand using either topspin or slice.

10. Can hit 3 out of 10 deep, slow bouncing balls on the rise with forehand and backhand.

Level 5 - Orange Serve and Return

1. Player can demonstrate a pro serve in slow motion.

2. Serve to opponents forehand and backhand in either court 5 out of 10 times while using the Continental grip using the safe serve position.

3. Serve 5 out of 10 using a Continental grip with a pro service motion.

4. Serve 3 out of 10 slice serves to both deuce and advantage court.

5. Serve 3 out 10 flat serves with full motion.

6. Serve 3 out of 10 topspin serves with full motion.

7. **Return:** Moves into court on server's toss, times split step to the strike of the ball, recovers horizontally to the center.

8. Returns 3 out of 10 second serves to the backhand court from deuce and advantage side.

Level 5 - Orange Overhead

1. Continental grip is the preferred grip on overhead.

2. Player can perform crossover and shuffle step on overhead.

3. Player can catch 7 out of 10 balls with off-hand out of the air.

4. Player can hit 5 out of 10 overheads out of the air.

5. Player can hit 5 out of 10 overheads off the bounce down the line and crosscourt.

6. Player can hit 3 out of 10 overheads off the bounce into all four quadrants.

Level 5 - Orange Volley

1. Continental grip has become the preferred grip for volleys.

2. Moves forward to volley.

3. Can hit 7 out of 10 forehand volleys from 5 feet behind the net.

4. Can hit 3 out of 10 forehand and backhand volleys from the service line.

5. Can hit 7 out of 10 coach fed approach shots down the line and finish with a forehand putaway volley while completing 2 split steps.

6. Can forehand volley 7 out of 10 short inside the service line.

7. Can forehand volley 7 out of 10 deep beyond the service line.

8. Can one-handed backhand volley 7 out of 10 coach fed volleys from 3 feet behind net.

9. Can hit 5 out of 10 catch volleys that are below the net.

10. Can hit 5 out of 10 high volleys by closing to the net and hitting down with power.

11. Can hit 5 out of 10 forehand volleys crosscourt.

12. Can hit 5 out of 10 forehand volleys down the line.

13. Can hit 3 out of 10 approach shots and finish with a backhand volley put away.

14. Can one-hand backhand 3 out of 10 short inside the service line.

15. Can one-hand backhand 3 out of 10 long beyond the service line.

Level 5 - Orange Lob

1. Can demonstrate the offensive forehand and backhand lob in slow motion.

2. Can hit 7 out of 10 drop fed backhand lobs from baseline and hit over the coach standing between net and service line.

3. Can hit 7 out of 10 coaches feed defensive forehand lobs over the coach standing between the net and the service line.

4. Can hit 5 out of 10 coaches feed defensive backhand lobs over the coach standing at the net.

5. Can hit 5 out of 10 coach feed offensive forehand lobs over the coach standing at the net.

6. Can hit 3 out of 10 coach feed offensive backhand lobs over the coach standing at the net.

Level 5 - Orange Game Understanding

1. Can play a match with no need of outside assistance.

2. Pass Orange Written Exam with 85% accuracy. (Study material must be requested from Kaizen Tennis).

Level 5 - Orange Character Development

1. Asks questions for ways to improve.

2. Always respects opponent by playing their best whether ahead or behind.

3. Begins to seek out competitive opportunities to play against more skilled opponents.

4. Understands how to stand their ground if the opponent is playing unfairly.

5. Beginning to understand the role momentum plays in a tennis match.

6. Beginning to understand the role confidence plays on their performance.

7. Feels genuinely good for the opponent when they play well and win.

Additional Levels

Levels 6 and 7 competencies and study materials will be available to the student once they reach level 4 red. Those levels are designated with the colors blue and brown. Levels 8 and 9 competencies and study materials will be available to the student once they reach level 6 blue.

Those levels will be designated with the colors purple and gold. Level 10 Black competencies and study materials will be available to the student once they reach level 8 purple.

The following are areas covered in future levels

Directional Tennis

How to Anticipate what is Coming Next.

Getting Off to A Good Start in a Match

Serve Routine

Self-Talk

Pre and Post Match Checklists

Matchplay Checklist

What it Takes to be Successful in Tennis

Qualities of a Great Tennis Player

Specialty Shots

Developing a Weapon

Being More Competitive

Dealing with Adversity

Singles Strategies and Priorities

Singles Tactic

Doubles Strategies and Priorities

Doubles Tactics

How to Play a Tiebreaker

How to Sabotage Your Opponent

Knowing what is Going on Across the Net

Sizing up Your Opponent

Neutralizing Your Opponent

How to Force an Error

Situational Tennis

Mental Tennis

Detaching

Emotional Tennis

SECTION IV

A Word to Parents

CHAPTER 15

Nine Reasons Tennis Increases the Quality of a Child's Life for Years to Come

Why take Tennis lessons?

I estimate that I spent 1,740 hours on a practice field with a coach playing football and about that much time playing basketball in high school. I loved it, learned important lessons, made friends, broke my leg, but finished on a high note with a successful senior season. The day I hung up my cleats at age 17 was the last day I received anything from all I had invested.

No longer would I receive physical fitness benefits, competition, recognition, status, social opportunities, or a resource for new friends. I wonder what if I had used that same time taking tennis instructions and playing more? I know I would have had more hours of fitness, playing, social interaction and success if I had put more time into tennis at an earlier age.

1. Inactivity is a Killer

The average young person today is underdeveloped physically as technology has increased and physical activity decreased. Most parents admit it is a battle to get their kids off technology even for a few minutes. This is a more significant threat that we may realize.

Technology is literally killing us. Recent studies by insurance actuaries show that life expectancy of children ages 6-12 is going down by 5 years due to medical issues arising from the tripling of obesity rates among this group due to inactivity.

The trends are alarming. Travel teams are causing a decrease in multi-sport players. There is less emphasis on physical education in schools, and at the same time, sports participation is declining. Seventy percent of kids dropout from organized sports after age thirteen.

See this illustration on the decline of youth sports between 2008 and 2013.

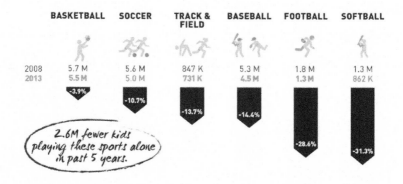

2. Tennis Can Improve Life

See below the added long-term benefits of an active and athletic lifestyle.

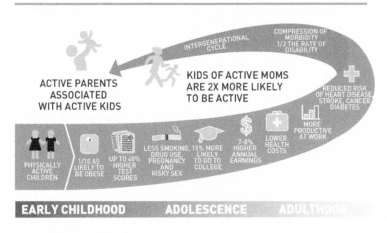

ACTIVE KIDS DO BETTER IN LIFE
WHAT THE RESEARCH SHOWS ON THE COMPOUNDING BENEFITS

3. Tennis is for Life

It is common for me to see players on the courts into their 80's. Few sports provide this kind of longevity. The desire to enjoy the game is ample motivation to keep a person active and in shape for years to come.

4. Tennis is Fun

Fun is a great motivator for our activities. Physical activities like running and weight lifting have great physical benefits, but many who have quit doing them have done so because they say they are just not fun. It is hard to discipline ourselves to do things we don't enjoy.

5. Skills developed in tennis will translate to many other sports and recreational activities.

The skills acquired in tennis translate to other sports as well as help them in many other ways to become a more confident and graceful individual.

The improved motor skills and hand-eye coordination will serve them for life, allowing them to excel in other recreational sports like golf, bowling, water and snow skiing, volleyball, etc. Improved motor skills give them tools for improving physical health and maintaining weight.

6. Tennis can make you happier

It has been proven scientifically that with physical exertion and competition the body releases endorphins, dopamine, and serotonin, all leading to a happier person with better mental health.

7. Tennis provides social opportunities

Tennis is a social game that can bring new and lasting friendships. If you develop a good tennis game, it will also build self-esteem and confidence while gaining the admiration of others.

8. Tennis is less expensive.

The initial cost of tennis is one of the least expensive of all sports. You can spend $40 - $200 on a racquet and $3.00 on a can of balls and you are good to go.

Only soccer and basketball are less expensive to get started. Contrast the cost of tennis to golf where a player must spend between $250 to $1500.00 for a set of clubs and between $45 to $150 on each round of golf.

Also, with the rise of travel sports, the cost of playing a sport can be significant. See below an article published by USA Today.

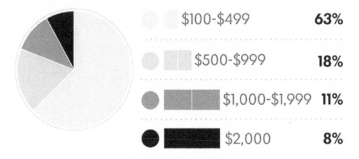

RISING COST OF YOUTH SPORTS
Nearly two out of 10 families are spending more than $1,000 per month on elite youth sports. Amount sports parents say they spend per child[1] on athletics:

$100-$499 **63%**

$500-$999 **18%**

$1,000-$1,999 **11%**

$2,000 **8%**

1 — If more than one child, percent shown reflects most expensive child
SOURCE TD Ameritrade
George Petras, USA TODAY

USA TODAY

Tennis, on the other hand, can be much less expensive. Even with the cost of lessons, monthly outlays can be manageable.

9. Tennis teaches character lessons.

Tennis has long had a reputation for being a game for ladies and gentlemen. From the way the game is set up, officiated, and scored it requires honesty and integrity. Many other life and character lessons can be learned from tennis.

CHAPTER 16

What Parents Should Know About Lessons

When Should a Child Begin to Play Tennis and what Should be the Goal?

Tennis should begin when the child's interest is peaked, and they want to play.

For young children, tennis lessons may not look too much like tennis, other than buying tennis clothes and holding a racquet and ball. The main goal of early sessions is the development of motor skills and tracking skills, but more importantly to introduce them to the idea that they are tennis players. Imprinting this idea early on can go a long way in their development.

Should Your Child Start with Group Lessons or Private Lessons?

The short answer is yes to both. Under age six, group lessons are best. If starting after age seven, most kids need more individual attention to help them learn the fundamentals of hitting a forehand, a backhand, a volley, and a serve as well as to learn the rules of the game. Private or

Semi-Private lessons are the best way to give them additional attention they need.

Before too long the student needs to learn how these lessons relate to playing the game of tennis, and here is where group lessons come in. **Group lessons** provide camaraderie and helps the student become comfortable with winning and losing in a competitive environment, which is very important in a person's development.

It is one thing to hit a tennis ball around and another thing to compete in a game. Kids react differently to competition. Kids with siblings or with similar age kids in their neighborhood are more accustomed and comfortable with competition.

Kids not accustomed to competition can feel a lot of anxiety with the thoughts of losing or not being good enough. One thing we do to counteract this is to have the kids play all sorts of games where there are a winner and loser, but without much ado about who wins or loses. I tell the kids all the time that winning or losing a game has nothing to do with who is a winner or loser, but is a test of your skills at that moment in time.

More importantly, there is something about competition that causes people to improve. I even hear professional athletes blaming poor performance on not being in competitive shape mentally or physically.

Private lessons are also needed from time to time as a player needs individual attention to work on different aspects of their game. The frequency of private lessons in some ways is dependent on how fast the student's ability allows them to grow. If the student has developed their athletic ability and are hungry for growth, then weekly lessons may be in order. For most kids, one or two lessons a month to supplement their group lessons is adequate to keep them on a positive growth curve.

Additional parent note: If the child is not showing a lot of interest in playing or practicing on their own, then I would not suggest private lessons at all. Kids play tennis for a lot of different reasons just as adults do. I frequently speak with adults who have little interest in improving their game, yet love getting out with their friends to enjoy fellowship, exercise, and competition.

Other Things Parents Should Know about Lessons

Tennis is not an easy game. A child who has not spent much time developing their athletic motor skills through other sports is likely to become frustrated. Developing the motor skills necessary to play takes time, effort and desire, but it is worth it. Patience is in order here. Going slow and building confidence is essential. An encouraging and patient parent is necessary.

Tennis is all about running and movement. With the inactivity brought on with excessive use of video games, your kids may resist games that require running and movement. You must remember they have become accustomed to staying indoors. Kids have become resistant to playing outdoors where it is cold or hot and they are not physically fit to endure it. This may be an obstacle you will have to push them through.

To play well, a child must practice between lessons to improve. However, some children do not have the temperament to practice alone. These kids may not practice unless they have someone with them to supervise and encourage like a parent or older sibling. If they don't practice between lessons, they stand a better chance of becoming discouraged as their progress will be slow.

Some children are more coachable than others. Some children want to do things their way. After a few lessons, it is a good idea to ask the coach if your child is coachable. If the coach says they are not, don't take it personally, but provide the coach insights about the child and what motivates her. Let the coach know that you are on their side for the benefit of the child. Communicate often with the coach and monitor the situation. If things do not improve, it may be time to look for another coach. Your child may respond differently to another coach.

Not all coaches are equal. Not all coach's personality will connect with your child. Just because someone is a good player doesn't mean they are a good coach. Talk to the coach and ask how your child is doing. A good coach will appreciate this.

Ask the coach what your child needs to do at home to continue improving. This prompts the coach to put forth more effort knowing he has your support once you leave the court.

The best tennis players are the ones who have at least one parent dedicated to seeing their child become a good player. It is a long process and requires consistency from the parent.

Group lessons alone are good and less expensive than private and semi-private. Group lessons are usually more fun for the student and provide opportunities for competition and match play, but there is not as much time for personal attention. A private or semi-private lesson in addition to group lessons are needed for best results.

CHAPTER 17

Growth Verses Fixed Mindset

Carol Dweck wrote a seminal book on learning called *Mindset*. In the book she identifies two mindsets she calls fixed and growth.

The fixed mindset sees accomplishment and learning as a fixed thing or talent. The child with this mindset judges himself and others by their current level or ability.

At one time or other, we have all done this. We see an accomplished pianist, and we think, "Wow, that person is really talented. They have a gift from God." What we don't see is the countless hours the person put into practice. We can't see all the beginner mistakes when this person began to learn.

The same goes for tennis. A new student begins to play tennis at age ten, and they see other ten-year old's who are already good tennis players. They assume this "good" player is talented and has a special gift. What they don't see is this child has been playing since they were six and taking lessons for four years.

The child with a fixed mindset will think; "I am either good at it, or I am not." "I can either do it or I can't." "My potential is predetermined." "I will quit and stick to what I know."

The child with a fixed mindset takes coaching as being critical. They take losing as being personal. When they get frustrated, they want to quit.

Children with this mindset often want to avoid competition, or if they do compete, they only want to play against players of inferior ability. To them, losing means they are a failure, instead of an opportunity to improve.

As a parent, you can either contribute to this mindset or work to change it.

The Growth Mindset

My favorite tennis player of all time is Roger Federer. He has won 100 professional titles in his career. When he was in his early 20's, he won three grand slam tournaments in one year.

They interviewed Roger after the third win, and he was asked what makes him play so well. He said, "When I was a boy, I never imagined that I could play this well. There are still several parts of my game that I can improve.

At age 37 he is still ranked in the top five of all players. When they asked him, "How can you continue to be so passionate about tennis after all your success?" He said, "I am still improving, and I see areas where I can continue to improve." This is the epitome of the growth mindset.

It is not easy to change the mindset from fixed to growth. It first takes the parent embracing the growth mindset. If you are reading this book, you most likely have a growth mindset. The growth mindset believes that we can always improve with enough desire and practice. We can continually improve no matter what it is we set our minds to, but it takes working at it.

Children with a growth mindset love to compete and see every opportunity, win or lose, as a way to improve. Actually, losing causes them to go over their performance in their mind looking for what they could have done better.

Reinforcing the Growth Mindset

When you wish to inquire about your child's game or practice, you might ask, "What parts of your game are you working on the most?" You might also ask, "Do you want to try anything new?"

When praising your child try to stay away from praising their talent or intelligence. Instead of reinforcing that talent or intelligence is fixed by saying you are smart or a good player; instead say, I can tell you are improving or, I liked the way you hustle after every ball, or you made good choices on the court today, or I like that you play hard on every point; whether ahead of behind.

All these statements reinforce the growth mindset and that they can continue to grow and improve.

Days When You Will Need to Encourage

There will be times when your child does not play well or plays a stronger opponent. You will need to encourage them. Here are some examples of things to say in those situations.

When You Child Suffers a Defeat

Example 1: Your child made a lot of unforced errors, but was giving good effort.

Your response: I really liked how you didn't give up going for your shots today.

Example 2: Your child just lost a close hard-fought match.

Your response: I am so proud of you and love that you are a such a fighter in a close game. These hard matches are going to make you even better in the long run.

Guarding against Complacency

Example: You child just won a lopsided match against a beginner.

Your response: If that player keeps practicing, they may be pretty good one day. You're ahead right now, but other kids are getting better too.

When Your Child Struggles with the Fixed Mindset

Most of us struggle with the fixed mindset from time to time. The following will help you identify when your child is struggling with it.

"I am not good at tennis."

"I can't hit a backhand."

"I have never won a match in competition."

All these objections your child has to their tennis ability are examples of the fixed mindset. These objections are all easily overcome with the **"Power of Yet."** View below examples of countering the fixed mindset with the growth mindset "Power of Yet."

"You are not good at tennis yet."

"You can't hit a backhand yet."

"You have never won a match in competition yet."

As you can see, all these responses assume the child will continue to grow and develop.

Final Word

The best thing that you can do for your child when it comes to tennis is to forget about the results. Results are uncontrollable, but the process is not. Focus on the process and be supportive. As part of the process, do your best to find a good coach that will teach good technique and at the same time make learning fun.

The primary goals for your child playing tennis are having fun, making friends, learning how to both win and lose and developing motor skills and tennis technique he will use for a lifetime.

I don't think I can emphasize enough the importance of learning how to win and lose. They are both imposters along the road of life. Feeling too good about winning and too bad about losing are both counterproductive. A better focus is on improving and developing a strategy to continue to improve.

Being a supportive parent is a delicate balance for sure. Here are a few ways you can help shape the process for improvement.

1. Find a good coach that teaches good technique.

2. Help locate a friend who can be a good partner for playing and taking semi-private lessons together.

3. Be consistent and encouraging with a growth mindset.

4. Observe whether or not your child is only playing others who are not as skilled. If this is the case, you might suggest they play someone in the area that would be a challenge for them or check out USTA tournaments in your area and suggest she play. If you get push back on this suggestion, it may indicate they are not yet confident enough or have a fixed mindset fear.

I hope you will enjoy your tennis journey as much as I have and have many years of fun and good health. If you have additional questions about any of this material you can email me at

Claiborne.mize@gmail.com

Made in the USA
Las Vegas, NV
28 April 2021

22187619R00080